Free Verse Editions

Edited by Jon Thompson

CANTICLE OF THE NIGHT PATH

WINNER OF THE NEW MEASURE POETRY PRIZE

Jennifer Atkinson

Parlor Press
Anderson, South Carolina
www.parlorpress.com

Parlor Press LLC, Anderson, South Carolina, 29621

© 2013 by Parlor Press
All rights reserved.
Printed in the United States of America
S A N: 2 5 4 - 8 8 7 9

Library of Congress Cataloging-in-Publication Data

Atkinson, Jennifer, 1955-
  Canticle of the night path / Jennifer Atkinson.
     pages cm. -- (Free Verse Editions)
  Poems.
  Includes bibliographical references.
  Winner of the New Measure Poetry Prize.
  ISBN 978-1-60235-356-5 (pbk. : alk. paper) -- ISBN (invalid)
978-1-60235-357-2 (Adobe ebook) -- ISBN (invalid) 978-1-
60235-358-9 (ePubf)
  I. Title.
  PS3551.T57C36 2013
  811'.54--dc23
                                        2012037950

Cover design by David Blakesley.
Cover art: "Botanical 71" © Sheep Jones. Used by permission.

Printed on acid-free paper.

Parlor Press, LLC is an independent publisher of scholarly and
trade titles in print and multimedia formats. This book is available
in paperback and ebook formats from Parlor Press on the World
Wide Web at http://www.parlorpress.com or through online and
brick-and-mortar bookstores. For submission information or to
find out about Parlor Press publications, write to Parlor Press,
3015 Brackenberry Drive, Anderson, South Carolina, 29621, or
email editor@parlorpress.com.

For all my teachers

. . . I said to him, 'Teacher, now does one who sees the vision
see it <through> the soul <or> through the spirit?'
The Teacher answered and said, 'One does not see through the soul
nor through the spirit, but the mind which [is] between the two—
that is [what] sees the vision and it is [. . .]

—*The Gospel of Mary [Magdalene]*

Permit me voyage, love, into your hands . . .

—*Hart Crane*

Contents

Canticle of A   3

Canticle of Assisi Rain   4

Canticle of Before   5

Canticle of the Bitter Almond Tree   6

Canticle of Blue   7

Canticle of the Bridegroom:
   from *The Parables of Mary Magdalene*   8

Canticle of the Cherry Tree:
   from *The Parables of Mary Magdalene*   9

Canticle with Chipped Plates   10

Canticle of Clouds   11

Canticle of the Crow   12

Canticle of the Day Path   13

Canticle of Dreams and Nightmares   14

Canticle of Dust   15

Canticle of the Egg in Magdalene's Open Hand   16

Canticle with Eyelashes   17

Canticle of the Fallow Field   18

Canticle of Fire   19

Canticle After Francis   20

Canticle of Francis, the Shepherd, and
   the Wolf of Gubbio   21

Canticle of the Gate   22

Canticle for Giotto's Magdalene   23

Canticle of Happiness   24

Canticle of History   25

Canticle of Hours   26

Canticle of Hunger   27

Canticle of If   28

Canticle of the Lavender Fields   29

Canticle with Ligurian Sea   30

Canticle with Macaroons   31

Canticle of Magdalene and the Lamp   32
Canticle for Magdalene's Outcast Demons   33
Canticle of the March-Blooming Mimosa Tree   34
Canticle on Matthew 6 in Wartime   35
Canticle of More Wishes   36
Canticle of the Naked Magdalene in Exile   37
Canticle of the Night Path   38
Canticle of the Orchard Owl   39
Canticle on Palm Sunday   40
Canticle of the Penitent Magdalene   41
Canticle for the Pilgrimage to Magdalene's Grotto   42
Canticle of the Pine in Her Garden   43
Canticle of Prayer Beads   44
Canticle of Quiets   45
Canticle of Rhymes   46
Canticle of the Rushes:
    from *The Parables of Mary Magdalene*   47
Canticle of St. Martha and the Dragon   48
Canticle with Secret   49
Canticle with Shrapnel and Manna   50
Canticle of the Sleeping Child:
    from *The Parables of Mary Magdalene*   51
Canticle of Slippage   52
Canticle of the Solution Cave   53
Canticle for the Sound   54
Canticle of Stone   55
Canticle of the Treasure Ship:
    from *The Parables of Mary Magdalene*   56
Canticle of the White Rose   57
Canticle of the Wolf   58
Canticle of Zed   59
Notes   61
Acknowledgments   63
About the Author   65
Free Verse Editions   67

CANTICLE OF THE NIGHT PATH

Canticle of A

An almanac of almost and almonds, amended accounts, always
  askance, aslant—ah!—as chance would have it;

An atlas, at last, of aphorism and aftermath, of master, ochre, mask,
  and umber, all had for an anaphoric song;

An archive of lives and ghosts, haloed and half-cocked; a canticle of
  alpha to zed, apple to zebra, aardvark to zarf;

A gospel of asters, of ask her, of azure assurance not gone askew, an
  adder, an attar of roses and ashes;

A Webster's of wishes, wordlists, of what ifs and why nots, wine
  cups kept ever brim full.

Canticle of Assisi Rain

An olive branch threaded with clear beads of rain.
The whole tree swagged with garlands of rain.

Fog, the same fog cowl Chiara wore,
That scarved her hair and shoulders, before, after, during the rain.

Pecking for crumbs in the gravel, fledglings
Hunch up and soften like bread in the rain.

The cypresses nod, a solemn quorum of elders,
A jury to rule on the rights of rain.

The lines of the city are washed away or left undrawn—
The road, wall, far side of the garden—forgotten, dissolved in the
    rain.

Canticle of Before

It has begun before it begins—with a foretaste, a bead of nectar, an
  unshed tear, glassine, brimming with impulse.

And before the bead: wind, before the wind: cold, before the cold:
  dark—an absence presence set aside, a hollow to harbor power.

And before the hollow: the hollowed, the whole, the indivisible
  one.

And before the one, the perfect zero: the knife that proves it flawless
  by flawing it.

And who holds the knife, subtle and sharp, the probe that pierces
  and then withdraws, leaving a single glistening drop?

6

Canticle of the Bitter Almond Tree

Is this spring—this gray-green net that snags the birds, this pruning
    hook—
Come now at last to wrest the almonds from their stupor?

Doubt is not irreversible, Love. Take care.

Without first the cold, the rehearsal of snow on the wet branches,
There are no blossoms or fruit—fruit kept for its hard pit, the flesh
    is cut away.

Almonds are just as much almonds at root, in leaf, as ash, as they
    are in blossom.

Will the feral cat, kinked tail twitching, a bird in her mouth,
Set it down to lap a dish of warm milk?

Canticle of Blue

Besides the scatter-light of empty sky, Tiepolo or Martin, domed
    illusion;

Besides the ocean's scribbled-on slate, weather's surface tricks and
    gambits;

Besides the beyond, the yonder, the shangri-la earth as seen from
    the moon;

Besides the wing, the crystal, the petal, the scale;

Beneath the robe of the holy, the veil, the nothing figured as shadow.

Canticle of the Bridegroom:
from *The Parables of Mary Magdalene*

It is like the ten girls who took their lamps and went to wait in the dark all night for a husband.

All grew drowsy: five blew out their lamps and slept, four trimmed their wicks to brighten their flames—they read to pass the time—and one stood up, snuffed her lamp, and walked out into the night.

The stars, unchallenged by lamplight, shone. In the air a rich fragrance of figs. The one bride plucked a ripe fig and ate.

All night the bridegroom never arrived. In the morning he called at the house of the wise and foolish. Look! Here is your bridegroom! Come out! Open!

But nine girls had risen, as always, at dawn to draw water. They were away at the well. The tenth, having returned from the well before daybreak, spoke through the closed door. Truly, I tell you, she replied, I don't—none of us knows you.

Canticle of the Cherry Tree:
from *The Parables of Mary Magdalene*

It is like a single cherry tree, surrounded with fences and growing in an orchard of cherry trees.

The fruit of the one tree is no redder or less red than the other trees' fruit. Where its bark has cracked, sap oozes out, forming amber beads that harden in place, mid-drip. In this it is like the other trees.

The separate tree's dusty leaves hang listless and bent, as do the leaves on the unfenced trees. All the cherries glow with late sun like jelly already put up in the jar.

Under the round shade of the fenced-in cherry, tall grass bleaches to hay, uncut and untrampled.

Come quick little foxes. Magpies come quick.

Canticle with Chipped Plates

I know you would appreciate the first-light sounds of off-key
bells, the pigeons singing like a stomach growling, the voices of
bricklayers joking as they walk past the widow's windows, while she
with her strong white arms flings open the shutters so they thud
and then thud just so against the walls.

I know you would notice the marbled swirl of silt eddied up after
each swallow of café crème, the mysterious landscapes of the spoon,
the shadow of the window sash bisecting a place mat.

You would never forget the wind slamming doors in empty rooms,
the bird who mistook a reflection for itself and fell, a spider swing-
ing on its lonely silk.

If you arrived today we would not speak. I'd boil a pot of the small
potatoes called *rattes* and serve them with hunks of butter and
salt—all alone on the chipped plates of our childhoods.

O the exquisite tears in the skins, the vortices of the dark eyes. To-
gether we will spear the smallest ones on our forks, apply butter and
salt. What other language would we need?

Canticle of Clouds

Stratus—stuff and nonsense;
                                    how things tear and frazzle;
A happenstance of riffle and spume; dust and diaspora; in short, the
    long view.

Cirrus—easy come;
                                    how things tendril, spindle, and tuft;
The ice- and milt-stippled current; a sigh; the intervention of drift.

Contrail—a stitch in time;
                                    how things linger and fade;
Legato passage, the having been; seam in the collateral damask.

Cumulus—two heads are better;
                                    how things swell and rush
To judgment; the hurly-burly of Moe and Larry; magisterial pomp,
    pratfallen.

Nimbus—see no, speak no evil;
                                    how things brim and spill;
Part and whole; the unmarked field over a field; pure radiance put
    to use.

Canticle of the Crow

For the sheer gloss of her   blacks, a gamut
Of darker-thans—hemlock,   skunk, junco's-eye,

Night rain   on paved roads.
For her wing's breadth,   her voice, her bravado,

The way she takes on   the wind wheeling,
The way she fits   in among lichen and human,

Key in the archway,   queen of the exurb,
Brooding her speckled   celadon eggs,

In flight, or unwinding   the life from the dead:
Alive O   praise her.

Canticle of the Day Path

I rouse myself from bed for a walk before breakfast. Look, I say.
  Listen.

Wild pears are blooming on the roadside. The stone mason's chisel
  isn't chink-chinking.

But I refuse not to sulk, refuse to meet the quiet halfway, to want
  more or less than coffee.

The road winds up the hill toward pealing bells, the polished cop-
  per light.

But coffee, hot milk! What could be better than coffee with bread
  and cold butter?

Canticle of Dreams and Nightmares

Of the baby who refused the breast, the one who never cried, the one found in the snow still sleeping, the one whose weight in my arms is my ballast;

Of the dove born through a chink in the wall, owls, crows as common as questions, the background noise of songbirds, sodden towels, the word *waterboarding;*

Of ladders, trapdoors, escalators into clouds, gates, padlocks, guarded exits, windows with sugar panes, a turret striped like a soda straw, climbing up and looking down;

Of not drowning, refusing to surface, liquid limbo, coming up shed of the human, floating face to face with the moon, finding a mirror, a mala, a knife at rest on the bottom;

Of hidden sunlit attics, unimagined chutes and shafts, a child crying behind the wall, rooms opening on opening rooms, tumbledown barns, caves, hollow trees, ships' holds charged with a dark that oozes like crude oil;

Canticle of Dust

Pollen, lint, scale, mites, mite shit, bits of skin and grit, residue and
shadow—light as light.

On air, aloft, feathered, furred, moted, de-moted, remote from its
sources—in motion.

Spume, fizz, fuzz, particulate substance of smoke, snow, crushed
bone, burnt bone—body ash, like beach sand but rougher.

Loess, silt, pumice, cloud, the glowering face of drought—the best-
kept secret of hail and rain.

Crop-, gold-, sandal, saw-, angel-, what you do with sugar—things
live, things dead, things not yet either.

Canticle of the Egg in Magdalene's Open Hand

Despite the stolen warmth, the stink of hen and straw, the
    pinfeather stuck to its crown;

Despite the polish, the rose-flushed brown, the fine pores and
    pimpled curves;

Despite the heft and rocking balance, the guise of all-knownness,
    the intact mask of once-but-now;

Despite the scarless, sutureless seal, the closed-box mystery, the
    ship-in-a-bottle, complete-in-a-teardrop shell;

The egg is more likely to ember, to redden, than ever to easter, to
    open alive.

Canticle with Eyelashes

The sod, the iris, the naked bones of the grapevines—the sorrow of
    things
I don't know either oppresses.

Resisting irony and comfort, sandaled in your reedy alto verses,
Telling a rosary of larvae and seeds, I'm tempted. Don't tempt me.

Whose words are not improvident, provisional, improvisational?

Summer sleeps in the autumn honey, in the hive's
Five thousand chapels of inwardness—sealed.

How can I answer you with your fistfuls of violets,
Dirt stuck to your lashes? I give up. What do you want, you owl of
    Christ?

Canticle of the Fallow Field

Bird shit isn't white because it's clean.
The fox isn't quiet from reverence.

Seed borne on the wind, seed cast among thorns, seed sown in rich
    or stony soil:
None thrives without the rain's reverence.

Queen-of-the-Prairie wears no crown and carries no scepter
Except by the moth's grace and the bee's droning reverence.

It's no good cursing the poppy for its ugly leaves,
The barley for its bitter root, the crow for its pious irreverence.

Winter comes. So does spring.
The ballet begins without overture, ends without the dancers' last
    reverence.

Canticle of Fire

Light layered in light—shelled, shellacked, sari-ed, mandorla-ed in
    ever lighter light.

Brilliance that blackens, that casts a dust shadow, that opens and
    shuts like an eye.

Heat that sings, that quiets, that's single and plural, conflagration
    and candle flame.

Body-spirit-mind edgeless, morphous, no more container than
    contained.

Red-tongued and panting, draped in the trees, a roar waits in its
    purr like a mine.

Canticle After Francis

For sister sun whose gold creates from vacant hours day,
For brother moon whose argent eye keeps watch all night,

For sister wind whose play delights and then destroys,
Whose storms fill cisterns and empty purses,

For brother water, spendthrift and miser by turns,
Who wields surrender like a broadsword drawn from a cloud,

For our brothers and sisters the creatures of earth and sea
Upon whose many mercies our lives depend,

And for sister death asleep in her cradle: when she wakes, before she
    thinks to cry,
Lift her from her swaddles. Press her cheek against your bared
    heart.

Canticle of Francis, the Shepherd, and the Wolf of Gubbio

Once upon a hill, a shepherd long ago and far away and a wolf of
what big teeth and slaver, lived alike on lamb, lamb bone, and
stars.

O they sang to the wax and wane, O to the glaring full.

Then came drought, came famine. Then snarled the wolf; the shep-
herd gnawed the gnawed bone then.
O they cried to the wane and wane.

So the stranger waved his hand: so rain, so corn. Sheep fat with
twins, one born for the shepherd live, for the wolf one stillborn.

O they sang to the wax and wane, O to the ever after full.

Canticle of the Gate

Such responsibility the gate takes on! To bar and to beckon, to preserve and to serve, to court and to thwart penetration!

The iron bars were wrought to look emaciated and arabesque like a dancer on point—that easily tipped over. O the elegant curliques and graces, the rays and arrows, the impossible symmetries of the spaces! But in its very delicacy resounds the stern clang of its essential nature. The gate cannot be breached without the key or a blowtorch.

You and I cannot pass through. The alley cat no one cares for (she does for herself by herself nicely) steps between the bars. The child, fearless with curiosity and disregard for the future, winkles herself under. But you and I are politely and firmly declined.

Beyond continues the same street, the same rain- and foot-worn cobbles, the same wood shutters at the windows painted the same shade of cerulean blue. Except—and it is an exceptional exception—we may never walk there.

Not at all and yet we wonder. Looking through, distanced by those torqued black lines the iron draws across the scene, we feel ourselves, our bodies change, our postures shift in response. The white cat turns her sleek head and stares.

Canticle for Giotto's Magdalene

Only until the rabbi's death does she succumb
To the painter's love of crushed cinnabar robes.

Afterwards veiled in salt and sleep, in a boat without mast or oar,
She lies down and lets St. Grief and green winds decide.

Naked, her every gesture refusal, she resists
Both black and white, both easy mourning and grave clothes.

Whatever she holds in her open hands—
Don't touch, don't ever touch—turns blood.

Carried over heaven's threshold, she surrenders
To the painter's need, gold leaf against his lapis field.

Canticle of Happiness

Why would you never, brother, self-tamed thrush, your lightning
   voice quenched
Like a sword in water, assent, and let joy, let pleasure, unhood your
   cage?

I yield you do for half a poem allow yourself a piecemeal gladness
But then you wrench it rough-cut away a quatrain later.

Before it can, though solitaire, be set, be diamonded,
You toss it down on thistled, stony ground like it's nothing—

A coin in a tourist fountain. A penny. The copper peace
On which I've spent my life, my love, and all my wishes.

A pocket-sized peace I can't help but hold, but thumb, but want—
For you too—a little low heaven in the blear-all black.

Canticle of History

In the wide realm of pine and cypress,
Wherever we rest our bed is green.

In the walled orchard of olives, wherever we walk,
We will walk, we have walked—

A labyrinth of unparsed tenses.

Hard earth underfoot, cold wind from the north,
Who needs the counsel of angels?

Among river willows or dry ridge lichens,
Wherever we turn we know where the path leads—

Canticle of Hours

Drizzle and dawn intermittent: a produce truck grunts and whines
    its way up.

Crows, pre-echoes, cronk-cronk from the tower: all four lift off just
    before the noon toll.

Rain, unburdened, gives way to sun: laughter spills from the
    school's opened windows.

Cracks in the glaze, flaws in the stained-blue light: the splash and
    warble of pouring wine.

Moonlight as if through a door left ajar: the high-pitched tick of a
    watch on the nightstand.

Canticle of Hunger

It is said she neither ate nor drank;

Or she lived on music, seven notes so rich in overtones
She couldn't, having swallowed them, consume a cherry more;

Or seven angels brought her seven bites—full moons turned
    edgewise,
Disks brittle as a wishbone, thin as an egg-white glaze;

Or she fed on manna that filled her mouth like spun sugar, manna
Dropped from the beaks of birds, one taste at each of the seven
    hours;

Or she took back her seven times seven pleas, gnawing and gnawing
    the gristle,
Until regret, regret, regret turned to honey in her mouth.

Canticle of If

I as if enthicketed: pine shade, pine needles and flinders, calm,
        Scratched calm, flit-flicker,
                  stopped light.

In the midst, the lapse, the fury, a seething buzz pressed to the verge
  of understanding:
        Like hearing voices if voices
                  prismed to silence.

Breathless, between breaths, impinged-on, light-stung:
        Self an if, in one stroke
             split open.

Say *if* and the shadows sublime to air:
        A text of live brightnesses, flight-
                  blurred wings.

Gasp and if will flare crested fire, beak and claw, instant and
  afterscent:
        Char, pine branch, the random
                  pulse of wind.

Canticle of the Lavender Fields

Under splotches of cloud-shadow and kiting cloud
A great dry lake of lavender.

Pine, honey, cut cork and sage, wheat
Scythed down and bound with wheat—the dry scent of growing
    lavender.

Monks' sung chants—unsequestered—brim over the sills
And spill out to water the dry lavender.

Who will walk with us among the furrows, the ruled waves,
Down the long dry voluptuous aisles of lavender?

Purple's woodwind timbre cools the throat,
Dry voices slaked and re-tuned to reedy lavender.

Canticle with Ligurian Sea

Into the intimate sea—secretive, bitter, viscous with memories held
    in suspense,

Into the phosphor, he sinks in slow-mo, dreamless, breathing dark.

His shadow hits bottom first, disturbs a fine confetti of wings, a
    moth-flight of silt.

Eugenio, look up. There it is, the shiftless, disassembled moon!

And see, good sir, beside it, the perfect O of your floating hat—

Canticle with Macaroons

Oh, Leopardi, you sad sack, buck up!

Enough of your wretcheds, dolors, sorrows, griefs, your born-to-
suffer, youth-to-wither arias to dying.

Seen through tears, what image doesn't wobble?

Doused with ash and raw vinegar, even the ripest peach turns alum
and sour.

Come, let me fill your mouth with kisses and amaretti. We'll set the
pretty wrappers on fire and let them fly off on flame wings.

Canticle of Magdalene and the Lamp

She feels your eyes like a blind man's fingers touch her contours, the fields of her face.

She has mused at the lantern for years, waiting, listening to the flame contend with a draft, a gust, a calm . . .

The skull rests in her lap like a baby, heavy, anonymous, mysterious as a newborn.

It is she herself who unbuttons her blouse, who vacates her alcove and opens her hands to you, to whoever comes and then departs.

She stands, pushes the chair flush with the table, and follows you, barefoot, treading too lightly to make a sound. Her hair, by now tangled and coarse, harbors moths and spiders and the smell of scorched milk.

Canticle for Magdalene's Outcast Demons

They were lambent, like firelight—
But cold, but dim;

Sheer, like silk—
But gray, but seven gradations of gray;

Hungry, like newborns—
But for bitter, for poison;

Refined, like gold leaf—
But leaden, tensile, untearable.

What could she do now, without their company to counter fear,
Without their counterweight and anchor?

Canticle of the March-Blooming
Mimosa Tree

It stands outside the walled garden of dove-belled cypress towers—

Its raw, rain-rinsed citrine blossoms too green, unsheathed,
   stripped, and sharp to look at long.

Inside, stone paths lead inward, if indirectly, to roses,

A sundial all day in shadow, a bench where someone dropped a
   glove.

Like dust, its pollen settles, faint in the veins of the cypress leaves.

Canticle on Matthew 6 in Wartime

Consider the missing lilies, the trees stripped of leaves and burnt, the grass trampled to dust.

Consider the crows of the air, what they reap, how they savor what others disdain.

Consider the splendor of kings, how they neither toil nor sow, and yet their coffers spill over.

Consider the empty barns and silos, the unplowed fields, the gravelly gnawing of hunger.

Consider tomorrow tomorrow: perhaps tomorrow will never come.

Canticle of More Wishes

For the dusk, salt, sour, summer-earth flush of a beloved's skin;

For oranges twisted and plucked from the tree, the silvery rustle of
   leaves—that scent;

For gnocchi browned in brown butter and sage, braised fennel
   with pecorino, broccoli with garlic and crushed red pepper, un-
   salted bread (that lonesome taste), and figs with vanilla whipped
   cream;

For a balm to be set on the torturer's tongue—ripe pear flesh
   dripping its honey;

For a balm to be set on the prisoner's tongue—ripe pear flesh
   dripping its honey;

Canticle of the Naked Magdalene in Exile

Defrocked, divested. Wrench loose the rudder,
Rend the sails. Let tide, let current, chart the course.

Unhooked, undone. Let the lace molder.
Let seed pearls fall where they will.

Magdalene slept under a flowering almond
And woke shivering, blotched with its petals.

A bee drank dew from her thigh.
One drop. One drop sufficed.

Suffices. Nakedness is penance
Is pleasure is penance.

Canticle of the Night Path

I want the moon to overfill, spill over, and drown me in dust light.
I want whatever happens after that.

I want the owl's one note to lull doubt to sleep.
I want to walk the night path.

Let the deer leap, the creek sing, the ferns loosen their infant fists, I
    promise I won't look.
Let the stars open like time-lapse roses, I promise to close my heart.

I want to taste the ozone, the fire-cleaved air, the acrid certainty of
    terror.
I want to be picked up and shaken.

Let day's slow fall, resistant as a single feather, be done.
I want what has nothing to do with wanting.

Canticle of the Orchard Owl

Voice from beyond the orchard walls,

Oracle or herself the god

Of walled almonds, of voles tunneled under

Moss, roots, wintercress—

Visible in retrospect as if by lightning

Canticle on Palm Sunday

Who sees the ash in the spark, the spark in the suede-soft ash?

Contained fire's naught but flimsy stuff, the ragged flag of a con-
    quered country,
A makeshift, ragtag pennant on a stick: *I surrender.*

Set loose in the wind, though, one flame leaps, turns legion, turns
    lethal,
Turns rush, a force five thousand shouts won't put out and can't
    muffle.

Who fuels a fire with green wood? Who beats it out with a dry
    stick?
And who reaches into the blaze twice to touch the dazzling embers?

Stop me, now, please, before I wish it, before I beg you, fire, come.

Canticle of the Penitent Magdalene

Even so the peaches are ripe, their pelts cat's tongue to my touch.

Even so the fierce poppies tremble.

Even so every night a dense blue like cold stones in my mouth.

Even so death rides the air, flitting and veering like bats, brushing
   my out-stretched arms, in passing.

Even so I dreamed the dream that Samson dreamed—honey oozed
   from a skull. The taste? Like honey. I poured it into my palm
   and licked.

Canticle for the Pilgrimage
to Magdalene's Grotto

For the long, rutted, washed-out path from the orchard to the
summit.

For the spring, just past halfway, where clear water pours,
Has always poured, cold from behind the stone.

For the trees—the resinous, revenant pines, the hard-scrabble
hollies, the oaks.

For the Sunday day-hikers, the monks, the woman crying bent over
her stick.

For the shadows at the end, deep in the cave, beyond the rule of sun,
Moon, candle or flashlight, the dark beyond imagining, where all of
us are drawn.

Canticle of the Pine in Her Garden

Sunlit at sunset, washed in late summer dust
    Ssplashed up from the valley,
                the pine is silent.

Blot on the star-pricked, star-smeared
    Sky after midnight,
              the pine is silent.

They called you Picasso's Magdalene, his Weeping Woman.
    After him, only God, they said you said,
                Dora of the silent pine.

The cicadas' choir loft, perch for the grief-voiced doves,
    Unless the wind comes by,
            the pine is silent.

It leans against the sky, at ease with falling, with looking down—
    Not only an image for the camera and canvas—
                Dora's silent pine.

Canticle of Prayer Beads

A mumbled bracelet, a cut-glass grammar of charms
Pierced through and linked in a sequence of rhymes.

Strung by rote, sung by heart: hailstone, vowel, hailstone.
Facets and cast refractions; prayer, pulse, drone.

Sounds cast before signs, a figure-eight of chime and plink:
Post hoc ergo propter hoc, post hoc ergo propter hoc.

A lariat of tangents and sequiturs, a round-and-round-she-goes
Of telling and told. Where she starts, she stops, where nobody
    knows.

The deictic clink of this against this, a synoptic gospel of what's left
    out,
A madam-I'm-adam of metaphor, a treatise of stop-gaps on doubt.

Canticle of Quiets

The first arises between deadfalls falling, one catbird's call and the
    next,
Between wind-stir and leaf-drop, birch-creak and ice-ring, birch
    and *birch*, ice and ring.

The second, only apparently so, is muffled jangle: sealed under its
    glass cloche
Fear breeds elaborate orchids—self-derision, self-contempt.

The third trembles—held fire: not yet, not yet, its beating heart.

The fourth is dumbfoundry, awe-strictness, over in an intake of
    breath,
The sound of a gas flame catching.

The fifth, the feared, the epilogue of expunged, is composed of the
    sighs of unhinging bone,
Sinew undone, the rhythmic friction of mandibles, organic
    chemistry 101.

Canticle of Rhymes

Bird with heard, burred, barred, br'er (briar), pair, wire, pine
warbler, water, war blur,

Egg with X, nest with *nide*, with need, knead, knees, heed with
hoard or hide nor hair or is it hare?

Talon with gallow, claw with crow, beak with break with beck and
call,

Wing with singe and song and thing with thing: like unfurling leaf
with fist-to-palm,

Quill with quail, quell, tail feather, ether, either, other, love or,
hover, power, forever and ever.

Canticle of the Rushes:
from *The Parables of Mary Magdalene*

It is like the widow who couldn't remember. Every day they sent her to the riverbank to cut reeds and canes with a curved knife. At dusk they led her back to eat bread and sleep.

Her dreams wove the reeds into baskets, which, before she woke, they sealed with wax and sent off empty, bobbing, on the river.

Every day she worked her way closer to the sea, each day beginning just right of the gap, just beyond the place she'd last left off cutting. As she cut, she hummed a song. She couldn't of course remember the words. As she hummed she sickled down the green canes and piled them neatly on the bank.

She worked until they told her stop, eat bread, sleep. She didn't know she slept to turn what grew into a bearer of what would grow.

She never spoke. Her palms, calloused by now, never bled. She didn't remember them ever bleeding.

Canticle of St. Martha and the Dragon

Words unacted on, like uncleaned, unscaled, unsalted fish, rot—a
  waste of breath and thought.

How could she kneel on the shore and pray when she might turn
  her back to the sea and walk?

What I do, she says, is who I am. And so she slew the dragon. She
  lanced its heart to still its flaming tongue and slashing tail.

As the fire left the monster's body, Martha plucked out its fang and
  with it cut her hair to weave a rope. With her hair-rope, she
  dragged the dragon into town for proof.

So, Martha the former kitchenmaid, sister of Lazarus the former
  corpse, was reborn St. Martha the Dragonslayer, savior of
  Provence.

Canticle with Secret

Of course you lived—you live—another dreamt life. Who doesn't?

Your words, meant to obscure, meant not to tell by telling else,
　　reveal in the negative space your secret.

The mountains and sulfurous lake, a lapful of petals and scalpels,
　　and not a word for ＿＿＿＿＿? White birch, burnt sail, the thin
　　broth of sunlight.

And what do you do now? A self-dissolving black thread of ants re-
　　stiches, re-sutures, the tear.

And what do you do after that? The next thing, dear heart, and the
　　next.

Canticle with Shrapnel and Manna

Stars in scattershot constellations recast themselves to suit us:
IED, Threat of Force, Bedazzlement after the Hood Comes Off.

Shards, singed bits and ash, flare-lit flak and shrapnel,
Hang in the blow-back, a missing-object lesson.

Saltine- and cake-crumbs dropped on purpose to mark the path
    back:
Why go back? Go back to what? The old stories are all about
    hunger.

Almond cakes, sweet with manna, flaky, dry aphid-honey,
Fed the people before the anfel, before the avenging bombs—and
    after?

Stars, moon, the night of our own invention underwhelms us,
Sheathe- and shelterless, not knowing who or what to trust, but
    looking up.

Canticle of the Sleeping Child:
from *The Parables of Mary Magdalene*

It is like a child asleep outside in her basket, shaded from late afternoon sun, veiled against evening flies, under her parents' loving watch.

Night is coming down, silently, like a worm on its strand of silk. The wind picks up.

Let me feed her before we go inside, the mother says. She says, *This feels like the last evening of summer.*

The wind is turning, faster now, like iron boring the hole in a millstone.

The father goes inside to fasten the shutters. The mother and the child at her breast are lifted skyward and set down unharmed, naked, in the temple courtyard.

Canticle of Slippage

She would like to rest just under the rained-on, distressed as-if-on-
　　purpose surface,
Irrelevant sounds quenched, light at a remove,

Time, like silt, suspended.

The sensation of dissolution, or is it absorption, into the water.
Gradually quiet quiets the banter, displaces the constant squabble,

The shilly-shall-I, will-I-won't-I nettlesome dither.

Such relief in surrender to prayer, tipping down
Slow through gradations of dark and still darker blue.

Canticle of the Solution Cave

Dissolving like sugar, like salt, the rock's hollow heart still widens.

Underground horizons exposed—pre-human and human centuries
marked in bars of gray and rust.

Blow out the rush-light: dark rushes close, a damp sweat slicks the
skin. As if a fever had broken.

Breathe the mineral air, blind, immersed in lightless not-knowing,
try not to be trying.

How foolish, sometimes, the longing for God—the longing and the
loneliness.

Canticle for the Sound

For rollick and slosh, salt bound and rebounding,
Its gallop, off-canter, and trot;

For cormorants, killdeer, eels, the half-fledged osprey trying
Its wings, the crab, the child—encastled, enmoated—rockweed;

For morning fogs that taste of decay, that cling, that cloy; for wind
Across the clear, for calm: one cloud—hand-in-glove, palm down;

For its welcome of rain, hailfire, slowfallen snow
Dissolved before— as—it touches down. For the clemency of its
    vastness.

For doxologies of the river mouth, the back and forth
One-word call and response of its tides—yes, it says, yes.

Canticle of Stone

An almanac of storms, spent rains, snows snowed and summers
   quenched;

A ledger of debts and excesses, each five billion lives compressed to
   a mineral glyph, a mere serif;

A glossary of mattes and glints, sift and flow, clench and thaw;

History told backwards, the score, the gospel of evolution, sutra of
   change, psalter of ante-, ante-, ante-;

Unplotted, un-authored, all ibid and op. cit., an endless dissertation
   on *on*.

Canticle of the Treasure Ship:
from *The Parables of Mary Magdalene*

It is like a ship with a cargo of treasure and a child alone at the helm—one child who is both captain and crew.

Bon voyage, the people shout from the dock. *Have a good trip!*

Far from shore, the child wakes up. He is thirsty, but he can't drink gold. He is hungry, but he can't eat jewels. *I am thirsty*, he says. *I am hungry.*

The ship, caulked, tarred, watertight, bobs like a seabird among the swells.

I wish I wish I wish, the child sings. *You wish you wish you wish*, the waves sing. And the child leaps singing into the sea.

Canticle of the White Rose

The lantern's shadow returns to its globe.

In the vineyards, summer's opaque clusters draw down the sun,
    crush daylight down to sugar.

Martins quicken, turn on edge and vanish, turn again and
    rematerialize blue.

Remember the rose, spindly, spending itself on one flower? Part the
    petals with your thumbs. There. There it is.

Night arrives as the silence after cicadas, the heady scentless blooms
    of plumbago.

Canticle of the Wolf

Trap-wise, trap-wary, surviving on oatgrass and fieldmice,
Gaunt, gray-at-the-muzzle, arthritic, the last wolf lies down,

Lifts her nose to read the wind's torn pages: snow, sheep's dung,
The just-turned earth, lamb's wool slick with amnion,

Inside, candle wick and honeyed beeswax, human sweat, lye,
Wool steaming dry by a fire . . .

She can hear the burning branch restage in flame its blooming.
She can taste in the smoke its seedy fruit,

Iron and floral, can translate the plosive whispers sighing
Down to ash to *is*.

Canticle of Zed

Does it stop—the zoetrope of over and over,
                              old and no older,
The carousel of next and next?

Zeno's half and half of half of halfway there,
                              that stuttered in-flight arrow,
The threat that never, seems never, will hit—

Let it. Not yet is getting too much to bear.
Love, give me your hand.

Zilch, zero's at-the-bone cold, the null
                              that slows the quick
In silver, the note, the hum, that mutes the tick, tick, tick,

Is ringing in my ears, a stuck song that needs
                              another to dislodge it—
Or is this the Without-which at last nothing is?

Notes

The Gospel of Mary [Magdalene] was among the damage-fragmented documents found at Nag Hammadi. I am indebted to the scholarship of many, but especially Karen L. King and Elaine Pagels, for their work on the so-called Gnostic gospels. I have relied on *The Nag Hammadi Library* as well as Susan Haskins's *Mary Magdalen: Myth and Metaphor* and Giotto's fresco cycle on Magdalene's life.

"Canticle with Chipped Plates" is for Jean Follain.
"Canticle with Eyelashes," for Salvatore Quasimodo, references several of his poems.
"Canticle of the Gate" is for François Ponge.
"Canticle of Happiness," for Gerard Manley Hopkins, borrows language from several of his poems.
"Canticle of the Ligurian Sea" is for Eugenio Montale.
"Canticle with Macaroons" is for Giuseppe Leopardi.
"Canticle of Magdalene and the Lamp" is for René Char, referencing his "Magdalen, Waiting" and "Madeleine with the Vigil-Lamp," itself after the painting by Georges de La Tour.
"Canticle of the Pine in her Garden" is for Dora Maar and Nancy Negley.
"Canticle with Secret" is for Antonia Pozzi.

Acknowledgments

Grateful acknowledgement is made to the editors of the following publications in which some of these poems—often in different forms—first appeared:

Beloit Poetry Journal, Cincinnati Review, Field, Free Verse, Image, Kaimana, Laurel Review, New American Writing, Not Just Letters, 2River View, St. Katherine Review, Spirituality & Health Magazine, Shenandoah, So To Speak, Witness.

The author would like to thank Nancy Negley and the Brown Foundation/Dora Maar House in Menerbes, France.

I'd also like to thank my many teachers (too numerous to name here!), Sheep Jones for permission to print her beautiful painting, "Botanical 71," on the cover, Susan Stewart, Jon Thompson, and David Blakesley, and several abiding friends and long-time readers without whose support and challenge I'd be lost: Katie Clare, Allison Funk, Carrie Grabo, Erin Kemper, Emily Lu, Melanie McCabe, Nadine Meyer, Emily Tuszynska, Toph Woodward, Peggy Yocom, and, of course and especially, Eric Pankey.

About the Author

Jennifer Atkinson is the author of four collections of poetry—*The Dogwood Tree, The Drowned City, Drift Ice*, and now *Canticle of the Night Path*, which recently won Free Verse's 2012 New Measure Poetry Prize. Individual poems have appeared in various journals including *Field, Image, Witness, New American Writing*, and *Cincinnati Review*. She teaches in the English Department and the MFA program at George Mason University in Virginia.

Phototgraph of the author by Eric Pankey.
Used by permission

Free Verse Editions

Edited by Jon Thompson

13 ways of happily by Emily Carr
Between the Twilight and the Sky by Jennie Neighbors
Blood Orbits by Ger Killeen
The Bodies by Chris Sindt
The Book of Isaac by Aidan Semmens
Canticle of the Night Path by Jennifer Atkinson
Child in the Road by Cindy Savett
Contrapuntal by Christopher Kondrich
Country Album by James Capozzi
The Curiosities by Brittany Perham
Current by Lisa Fishman
Divination Machine by F. Daniel Rzicznek
Erros by Morgan Lucas Schuldt
The Forever Notes by Ethel Rackin
The Flying House by Dawn-Michelle Baude
Instances: Selected Poems by Jeongrye Choi, translated by Brenda Hillman, Wayne de Fremery, and Jeongrye Choi
A Map of Faring by Peter Riley
Physis by Nicolas Pesque, translated by Cole Swensen
Poems from above the Hill & Selected Work by Ashur Etwebi, translated by Brenda Hillman and Diallah Haidar
The Prison Poems by Miguel Hernández, translated by Michael Smith
Puppet Wardrobe by Daniel Tiffany
Quarry by Carolyn Guinzio
remanence by Boyer Rickel
Signs Following by Ger Killeen
These Beautiful Limits by Thomas Lisk
An Unchanging Blue: Selected Poems 1962–1975 by Rolf Dieter Brinkmann, translated by Mark Terrill
Under the Quick by Molly Bendall
Verge by Morgan Lucas Schuldt
The Wash by Adam Clay
We'll See by George Godeau, translated by Kathleen McGookey
What Stillness Illuminated by Yermiyahu Ahron Taub
Winter Journey [Viaggio d'inverno] by Attilio Bertolucci, translated by Nicholas Benson